Pictorial Weavings
of the Navajo

Nancy N. Schiffer

D1254818

1469 Morstein Road, West Chester, Pennsylvania 19380

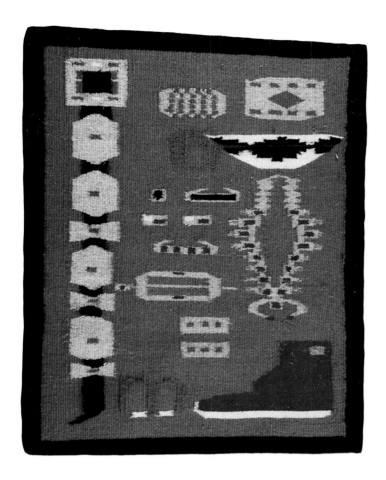

Typical Navajo silver jewelry on a pink background. Woven by Doris Peshlakal, 1990. 21" x 18". Courtesy, Shiprock Trading Company.

Photographs of landscapes on Navajo lands by H.L. James. Photographs of the objects by Douglas Congdon-Martin, Herbert N. Schiffer and Peter N. Schiffer.

Copyright © 1991 by Schiffer Publishing, Ltd.
Library of Congress Catalog Number: 90-60955.

Printed in the United States of America.
ISBN: 0-88740-318-2

Published by Schiffer Publishing, Ltd.
1469 Morstein Road
West Chester, Pennsylvania 19380
Please write for a free catalog.
This book may be purchased from the publisher.
Please include $2.00 postage.
Try your bookstore first.

We are interested in hearing from authors
with book ideas on related subjects.

Title page photo:
Landscape weaving of exceptional quality with a complicated design showing a Navajo family in various activities of domestic life. Woven by Linda Nez. 56½" x 40½". Courtesy, Theda and Michael Bassman.

Front cover:
Landscape weaving showing grazing animals and a Navajo family engaged in several occupations: shearing wool, silversmithing, and weaving on an upright loom. The detail is very sharp and colors full of variety indicating a very accomplished weaver. Woven by Laura Nez, 1990. 42½" x 58". Courtesy, Private collection on permanent loan to Ohio University.

Back cover:
Eight landscape designs arranged in a Storm Pattern. Woven by Gladys Richards, 1973. Courtesy, Dennehotso Collection.

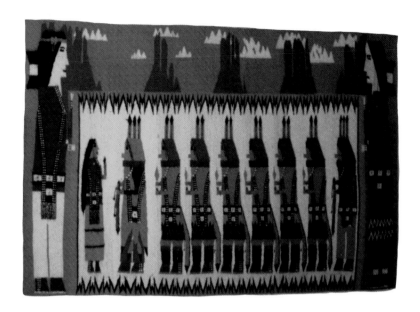

Wonderfully imaginative weaving showing a Yei bi chei dancers pictorial design within a landscape and two people. Courtesy, Foutz Trading Company.

CONTENTS

Pictorial weaving of the Navajo nation seal. Woven by Gladys Richards. Courtesy, Private Collection.

Weaving of the Navajo nation seal. Woven by Bessie Hadley, 1990. 20″ x 30″. Courtesy, Kiva Indian Trading Post.

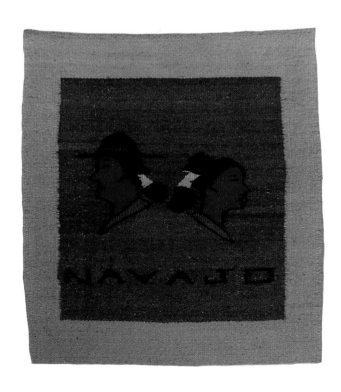

Pictorial labeled "Navajo" with the faces of a man and a woman with Navajo hair styles. Woven with natural wool by Ruth Cly, 1976. 25½″ x 23¼″. Courtesy, Private Collection.

INTRODUCTION

The Pueblo inhabitants along the Rio Grande River in Northern New Mexico were weaving cotton before the arrival of Spanish sheep in the sixteenth century. Into this arid and mountainous land the Navajo people migrated and learned to weave from their new neighbors. Early weavings are so rare that mere traces of original patterns exist to tell us little of the size or uses of the cloths. But by the time white people contacted the Navajo they were proficient at weaving blankets with horizontal bands of natural and vegetal dyed colors.

As the United States expanded into the Southwest during the nineteenth century, examples of high quality Navajo weavings were recorded. Blankets were either "finely woven and thin (famous for being waterproof,) or soft and loosely woven. There was very little weaving of the middle quality."[1] The blankets became trade items and when the system of traders became established at the end of the century, the weavers were encouraged to make heavier goods to be sold in the East as rugs, not blankets.

Representations of recognizable objects occasionally have been designed into Navajo weavings at least since the middle of the nineteenth century. Early extant examples show small bird figures in the regular Navajo geometric designs. The frequency of these life-like representations (these pictorial images) appearing increased when the Navajo people returned to their homelands from an internment at Bosque Redondo (1864-1869.) Still rare, but increasing in frequency, pictorials emerged to include images of everyday life, animals, landscapes, spelled-out words, and even ceremonial significance. When tourists appeared on Navajo lands, pictorials were seen as charming and so traders, particularly those in the northern reaches of the reservation lands, encouraged their being made. From the Farmington, New Mexico area in the east, to

[1] Rodee, M. *Weaving of the Southwest*. West Chester. Schiffer Publishing. 1987. p. 65.

Example of an early pictorial duck and weasel weaving. Circa 1900-1920. Natural grey and white Merino wool and synthetic dyed black and red. 69" x 47½". Courtesy, Dewey Galleries, Ltd.

beyond Dennehotso and Keyenta, Arizona in the west, and from the "Four-corners" in the north to the Lukachukai mountains in the south, Navajo weavers became adept at weaving pictorial images.

The categories of pictorials which comprise this work demonstrate the weavers' versatility and imagination which is wide and deep. Today, pictorials comprise a growing segment of Navajo rug production, and new designs continue to be woven. The evolution of this art form continues.

Pictorial weaving with Masonic emblems. Circa 1900-1915. 53″ x 33″. Courtesy, Dewey Galleries, Ltd.

Pictorial weaving of four snakes with a raised outline border. Circa 1910-1920. 53½″ x 74″. Courtesy, Lynn Trusdell.

SECULAR DESIGNS

Pictorial weaving with two cow heads. Circa 1930. 84" x 52". Courtesy, Dewey Galleries, Ltd.

Double Saddle blanket inspired by a McGuffey's spelling book, circa 1920, 48" x 24". Courtesy, Crown & Eagle Antiques.

Animals

Real and imaginary, local and exotic

Weaving with a delightful variety of animals in a night scene with black background. Woven by Effie Black, Lukachukai, 1956. Courtesy, Private Collection.

Animal patterned pictorial weaving with a bold geometric key in the border. The animals include domestic and wild types curiously grouped around a Navajo hogan. Surely this was a weaver's dream. 1974. Courtesy, Private Collection.

Yellow pictorial weaving with animals. Is this the daytime view of the zoo? Woven by Effie Black, Lukachukai, 1976. Courtesy, Private Collection.

Two horse heads and a cow head on this weaving. Woven by Florence Henio, Ramah, New Mexico. 37″ x 20½″. Courtesy, Kiva Indian Trading Post.

Weaving of three horses in a stark, almost Art Deco style arrangement with an outlined border. Courtesy, Foutz Trading Company.

Animal pictorial weaving of man and his horse. Woven by Ruth Harvey. Courtesy, Private Collection.

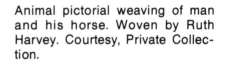

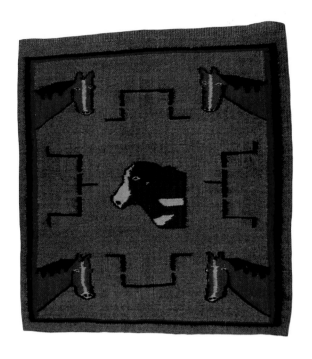

Charming pictorial weaving of men practicing rodeo stunts in the open range, roping and bronco and bull riding. The border treatment is unusual. Courtesy, Foutz Trading Company

Animal pictorial weaving with four horse and one cow head. Woven by Ilene Keith. Courtesy, Private Collection.

"Brownhorse." Is that his name or an accurate description? Only the weaver knows now. 1940s. Courtesy, Dewey Galleries, Ltd.

Animal pictorial weaving of a black horse and corn plants. No border here. Woven by Effie Black, Lukachukai, 1976. Courtesy, Private Collection.

Animal pictorial weaving showing a pleased cowboy after roping a calf. Woven with commercial yarn by Susie Whiteship, 1974. Courtesy, Dennehotso Collection.

Horse and rider pictorial weaving with lots of action. Circa 1975. Woven by Susie Whitesheep. Courtesy, Private Collection.

The action is keen for this bronco-buster! Pictorial weaving with geometric border. Courtesy, Private Collection.

Animal pictorial weaving of green-shirted men roping calves. Woven by Effie Black, Lukachukai, 1976. Courtesy, Private Collection.

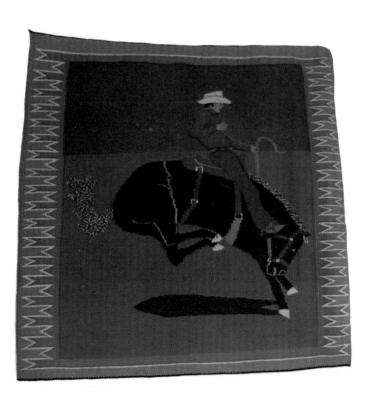

Rodeo rider in a precarious position on this pictorial weaving. The spectator should step to the left so he won't be run over. Woven with processed wool yarn and cotton warp by Mary Joe, 1971. 19" x 29". Courtesy, Dennehotso Collection.

Pictorial weaving with a bold outlined border and central diamond, bronco riders and three horse heads in the center. Circa 1975. Woven by Vida Joe. Courtesy, Dennehotso Collection.

Rodeo. Tension and interaction between the figures is clearly evident in this great design. Woven by Helen Chee, 1990. 31" x 42". Courtesy, Shiprock Trading Company.

On Safari!

Exotic animal pictorial weaving which conveys the magical quality of spirit forces. Circa 1970. Woven by Lena Zelth. 38″ x 24″. Courtesy, Private Collection.

Two elephants waving their trunks. Woven by Fannie Pete. 29″ x 22″. Courtesy, Dewey Galleries, Ltd.

Weaving of a kangaroo eyeing a butterfly. Woven by Fannie Pete. 31″ x 19″. Courtesy, Kiva Indian Trading Post.

Seated lion pictorial. Woven by Fannie Pete. 31″ x 23½″. Courtesy, Kiva Indian Trading Post.

Even a pig pictorial weaving. Courtesy, Kiva Indian Trading Post.

The delightful Raccoon Ranger personification and his bear friend. Woven by Ida Smelt. Courtesy, Dennehotso Collection.

Tigers at play, the design inspired by a picture in a magazine. Woven by Minnie Francis, 1990. 36½″ x 53″. Courtesy, Shiprock Trading Company.

Brown bear and his mountain friends in an expansive landscape setting. Woven by Betty Nez, 1988. 33¼" x 40¾". Courtesy, Private Collection.

Animals in a landscape with an unusual commercial dyed purple border. Woven by Lucinda Nez. 32½" x 29½". Courtesy, Foutz Trading Company.

The evil "Skin Walker" theme of this weaving is portrayed in exotic symbolism of spiritual significance not well understood by non-Navajo people. It was a daring subject to attempt. Woven with handspun natural and aniline dyed wool, 1990. 41½" x 48½". Courtesy, Private collection on permanent loan to Ohio University.

Birds

Subtle bird and lizard motifs woven within brown geometric shapes and a bold border. Circa 1915-1925. 59" x 41½". Courtesy, Dewey Galleries, Ltd.

Bird design pictorial weaving within a Teec Nos Pos style border. Circa 1925-1935. 56" x 33". Courtesy, Dewey Galleries, Ltd.

Early pictorial weaving showing four roadrunners, bows and arrows within a border. Circa 1920-1940. 87" x 57". Courtesy, Lynn Trusdell.

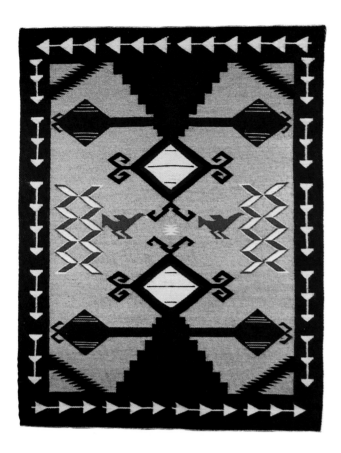

Brown and black pictorial of five eagles in an elaborate double border. Woven by Vida Rose Joe, 1980. Courtesy, Dennehotso Collection.

Pictorial weaving with three eagles and a rabbit, made with processed and commercial wool. Woven by Vida Rose Joe, 1973. Courtesy, Dennehotso Collection.

Geometric-designed weaving with two blue birds, probably inspired by a design from about 1900. This weaving by Marilyn Yazzie, Ganado, 1990. 48" x 36". Courtesy, Kiva Indian Trading Post.

Pictorial with a single dominant eagle in a landscape design and figured border. Woven by Lillian Smiley, Rock Point, 1976. 27" x 28". Courtesy, Dennehotso Collection.

The American symbol of freedom is conveyed by this weaving of an eagle and a rock, "USA" in the clouds. 1990. 23″ x 20″. Courtesy, Kiva Indian Trading Post.

Watch out rabbit! A magnificent flying eagle is shown in pursuit of a running rabbit. Woven by Wilson Gray, 1966. Courtesy, Private Collection.

Three dominant brown eagles share the field with various reptiles and animals on this ambitious weaving. Circa 1975. Courtesy, Dennehotso Collection.

Pictorial weaving of a flying eagle preying on a chicken and chick. 23¼″ x 15½″. Courtesy, Private Collection.

Eagle pictorial weaving with friendly birds in attendance. Woven by Mary Begay. 17″ x 14¾″. Courtesy, Private Collection.

"Bird Thunde" pictorial weaving. Woven by Ella Begay. 18″ x 16″. Courtesy, Private Collection.

Eagle and arrows design with horizontal bands. Woven by Sarah Travis, Kayenta, 1973. Courtesy, Private Collection.

Butterflies

Small weaving of a butterfly and wild flowers, 1990. 19½″ x 17″. Courtesy, Kiva Indian Trading Post.

Natural grey and white wool pictorial weaving with flying eagle and butterflies within a strong geometric block pattern. Woven by Vida Joe. Courtesy, Dennehotso Collection.

Pictorial weaving which combines a geometric diamond design with butterflies, all within an outlined border. Courtesy, Foutz Trading Company.

Vegetal dyed pictorial weaving with a butterfly and wild flower pattern in rows. Woven by Natalie Nelson, Chinle, 1984. 50″ x 35″. Courtesy, Kiva Indian Trading Post.

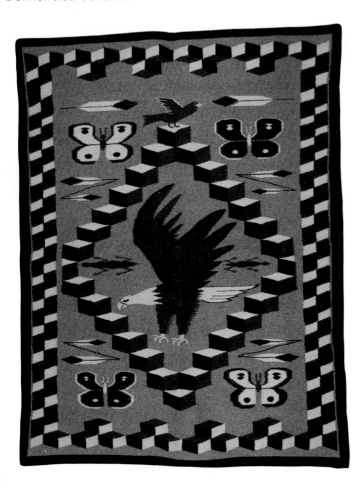

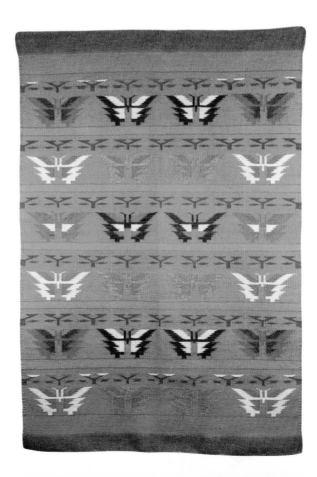

Landscapes

Early pictorial weaving of Ganado style with four U.S. army-style buildings and flags. Courtesy, Dewey Galleries, Ltd.

Pictorial weaving in the Ganado style with four white man's style buildings, animals, people, pine trees, and stars. Woven with natural and aniline dyed handspun wool. Circa 1920. 58" x 42". Courtesy, Private Collection.

Pictorial landscape designed weaving of the "Dennehotso Trading Post" in its remote landscape with vehicles, animals, and two medicine baskets. Woven by Jane Brown, 1973. Courtesy, Private Collection.

Pictorial weaving of the "J.L. Hubbell Trading Post, Ganado, Arizona" building and yard. Woven by Marjorie Hildroth, Steamboat, Arizona, early 1970s. 33" x 44". Courtesy, Hubbell Trading Post.

Weaving with labeled "house" and "cow" design. Woven by Edith Begay. 13½" x 10". Courtesy, Shiprock Trading Company.

Pictorial landscape labeled "Oh What Day" with rock formations, hogan, tree and sheep. Woven by Julia Tom, 1990. 13¼" x 11¾". Courtesy, Shiprock Trading Company.

Pictorial landscape labeled, "Have a nice day" with truck, highway, and cows by a pool of water. 16¼" x 14". Courtesy, Shiprock Trading Company.

Pictorial landscape labeled, "The Old Man Down the Road" in the rock formations. Woven by Julia R. Tom, 1990. 16½" x 14". Courtesy, Shiprock Trading Company.

Landscape with a buffalo hunt and one rider riding backward. Woven by Jessie Begay. Courtesy, Dennehotso Collection.

Beautifully shaded landscape weaving with geometric patterned border labeled, "Monument Valley Utah". Courtesy, Foutz Trading Post.

Monument Valley landscape of commercial yarn and wool warp. Woven by Etta Steve, 1972. Courtesy, Dennehotso Collection.

Landscape with Plains tribe hunting scene and two pine trees. Woven by Joanne Goat. Circa 1975. Courtesy, Private Collection.

Small winter landscape weaving of
a Navajo home setting. Courtesy,
Foutz Trading Company.

Summer landscape with tractor,
green field, silo and barn, and some
strange farm animals. This Navajo
weaver has imagination! Woven by
Mary Stanley. Courtesy, Private
Collection

Landscape with four hunters, small
pine trees and rocky ground. Woven
with commercial yarn and cotton
warp by Susie Whitesheep, 1974.
28″ x 31″. Courtesy, Dennehotso
Collection.

Distant mountain landscape with large tepees and a significant mountain stream, perhaps a scene in Montana. Woven with commercial yarn by Betty Yazzie, 1973. 26″ x 29″. Courtesy, Dennehotso Collection.

Southwest landscape with rock formations, animals, and rugs airing on a bar. Woven by Mary Labato, 1971. 41″ x 32½″. Courtesy, Private Collection.

Mountain meadow landscape with Navajo family and hogan, commercial wool. Woven by Isabel John, 1970. 26″ x 39″. Courtesy, Dennehotso Collection.

Landscape with goats and a Navajo family homestead. Woven by Billie Chee Gray, 1974. 38½″ x 37″. Courtesy, Private Collection.

Landscape weaving with rock formations and storm clouds, no border. Woven by Alice Blackwater. Courtesy, Private Collection.

Pictorial weaving with a Rainbow Yei figure surrounding three sides of a farm landscape, including a busy Navajo family. Woven with commercial yarn by Ruth Tsosie, Shiprock. 32″ x 32″. Courtesy, Dennohotso Collection.

Landscape pictorial showing animals in a farm yard with man, pickup truck and well head. Woven by Ruth Tsosie, Shiprock. Circa 1980. Courtesy, Private Collection.

Mountain landscape with stream, animals, and purple clouds. Woven by Alice Blackwater. Circa 1975. Courtesy, Private Collection.

Landscape with large brown tree and horses grazing below it. Woven by Jane Brown. Courtesy, Private Collection.

Landscape designed weaving of a shepherd. Woven by Mary Stanley. Courtesy, Private Collection.

Landscape with two children on a cliff. Woven by Valencia Nez, Chinle, Arizona. 23″ x 24″. Courtesy, Hubbell Trading Post.

Landscape weaving with two trees, four hogans, many animals and people, within a bold border. Woven by Norma Harrison, 1978. 46½″ x 34½″. Courtesy, Private Collection.

Modern times! The cows in this landscape are startled by their noisy invader, a helicopter! Woven by Marie D. Anderson. 36" x 41". Courtesy, Kiva Indian Trading Post.

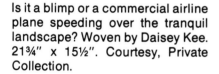

Is it a blimp or a commercial airline plane speeding over the tranquil landscape? Woven by Daisey Kee. 21¾" x 15½". Courtesy, Private Collection.

Finely detailed landscape weaving with five people in different occupations: cooking, silversmithing, spinning wool, weaving, and tending sheep. Woven by Florence Riggs, 1990. 35" x 42½". Courtesy, Foutz Trading Company.

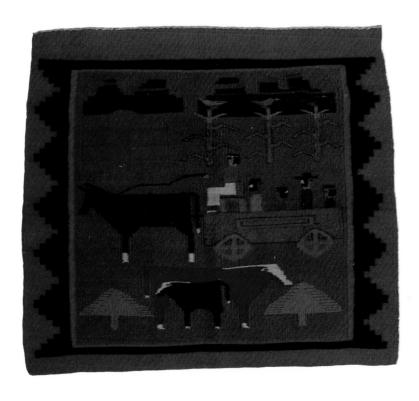

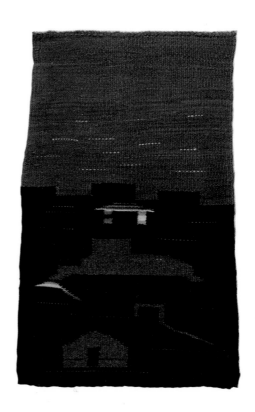

Weaving with buckboard and farm landscape, commercial wool and cotton warp. Woven by Bertha Charley, 1972. 26" x 30". Courtesy, Dennehotso Collection.

Night landscape weaving without a border. 26¼" x 17¼". Courtesy, Private Collection.

Landscape with trailers, vehicles, and a train. Woven by Ella Jean. 39" x 29". Courtesy, Hogback Trading Post.

Grey landscape design with a train. 20½" x 27½". Courtesy, Lynn Trusdell.

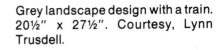

Old style geometric Ganado pattern, based on the Chief design, but with the addition of pictorial figures and trains. Woven by James Joe, 1990. 60″ x 49½″. Courtesy Foutz Trading Company.

Landscape pictorial weaving with unusually compartmentalized color areas. Corn plants, bears and birds are separated by the background changes. Woven by Susie Harrison. Courtesy, Private Collection.

Landscape weaving with hard-edge color divisions and overlapping figures. Woven by Sarah Brown. Courtesy, Private Collection.

Reservation Roads

Typical roadside landscape of the Southwest in a pictorial weaving by Louise Nez. 30½″ x 53″. Courtesy, Private Collection on loan to Ohio University.

Pictorial landscape labeled, "Country Road Take Me Home" with a hitchhiker, roadway, and typical Navajo farmstead. Woven by Julia Tom. 28½″ x 30½″. Courtesy, Shiprock Trading Company.

Inspired by the popular song by John Denver of the same name is this pictorial landscape labeled, "Country Road Take Me Home" with four medicine baskets, a hitchhiker, roadway, and pasture. Circa 1985. Courtesy, Foutz Trading Company.

Roadside landscape with a Coors beer truck labeled, "Keep on Truckin". Woven by Ella Begay. 13" x 14¼". Courtesy, Shiprock Trading Company.

Roadside landscape with vehicles and fuel pumps. Woven by Fannie Mann, 1979. 88¼" x 69". Courtesy, Private Collection.

Roadside landscape with people gathered for a Navajo ceremony. Woven by Emma Nez. 84" x 52". Courtesy, Foutz Trading Company.

Landscape with vehicles, an oil rig, and cowboy roping a calf. Woven by Gladys Richards, 1973. Courtesy, Private Collection.

Pictorial landscape with two pick-up trucks, animals, and unusual purple border. Round Rock area. 34″ x 21½″. Courtesy, Private Collection.

Modern roadside landscape with three jet planes flying by. Woven by Ella Begay. Courtesy, Foutz Trading Company.

End of the Trail

"End of the trail" rider with Plains headdress saluting the unseen gods. Woven by Jean Ann Goat, 1966. Courtesy, Dennehotso Collection.

"End of the trail" rider honoring a sky spirit. Woven by Ruth Tsosie, Shiprock. Courtesy, Private Collection.

"End of the trail" design with black border. 29" x 35". Courtesy, Keams Canyon Arts and Crafts.

"End of the trail" pictorial weaving without a border. Woven by Lillian Begay, 1970. Courtesy, Dennehotso Collection.

RELIGIOUS DESIGNS

Storm Pattern

The first mention of the Storm Pattern appears to be J.B. Moore's 1903-1911 catalog where Plate XXVIII shows a central rectangle joined to four corner squares by stepped lines. The catalog description claims "The pattern is one of the really legendary designs embodying a portion of the Navajo mythology."

This weaving is remarkably similar to J.B. Moore's plate IX of a catalog published some time between 1903 and 1911, with the addition of a human figure at the center. The Storm Pattern is marked in black. 91" x 55". Courtesy, Lynn Trusdell.

Brown animals and birds and a Storm Pattern on a grey background. Circa 1975. Woven by Pauline Black. Courtesy, Private Collection.

Weaving with central Storm Pattern crescent moon and stars. Circa 1915-1925. 45" x 23". Courtesy, Dewey Galleries, Ltd.

Four cars and a building (garage?), corn plants, and rock formations including "Window Rock," in a Storm Pattern. Woven by Julia Pete, 1983. 42" x 30". Courtesy, Kiva Indian Trading Post.

Pictorial weaving of two Yei figures and a horse in a Storm Pattern. Woven by Ruth Harvey. Courtesy, Private Collection.

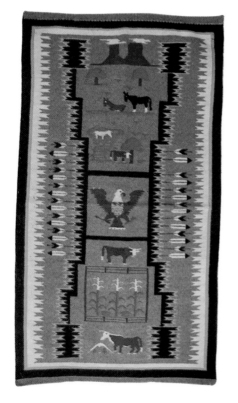

Storm Pattern pictorial with landscape scene. Circa 1975. Woven by Edna Joe. Courtesy, Private Collection.

Pictorial weaving with Storm Pattern, American eagle, and landscape with animals, made with processed yarn. Woven by Susie Speck, 1973. 28" x 49". Courtesy, Dennehotso Collection.

Raised outline weaving, pictorial Yei figure, Storm Pattern, and corn plant. Woven by Doris Haskan. Circa 1975. Courtesy, Dennehotso Collection.

Christian Ceremonies

Small weaving showing Jesus and the Last Supper. 14″ x 18″. Courtesy, Dewey Galleries, Ltd.

"Happy New Year" with decorated pine tree. Woven by Daisy Kee. 28″ x 18½″. Courtesy, Foutz Trading Company.

Weaving showing Christmas-related objects. Circa 1985. Courtesy, Foutz Trading Company.

"Merry Christmas" weaving with candy canes, bells, Santa Claus, and decorated pine tree. 1985. Courtesy, Foutz Trading Company.

Navajo Ceremonies

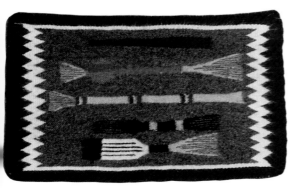

Weaving showing instruments for Peyote religious ceremonies. Woven by Doris Yazzie. 17½" x 10¼". Courtesy, Foutz Trading Company.

Pictorial weaving with implements for a Navajo religious ceremony and two men. Woven by Elsie Begay, 1973. Courtesy, Private Collection.

"Merry Christmas" weaving which shows a Christian Christmas tree and Santa with Navajo medicine basket and piles of food. The combination of cultural influences is a typical Navajo adaptation. Courtesy, Foutz Trading Company.

Religious ceremonial implements featured on this pictorial weaving. Circa 1985. Woven by Joann Goat. Courtesy, Private Collection.

People

Very early pictorial with traditional horizontal, natural, and aniline dyed bands and a pictorial of the Navajo religious figure, Changing Woman, a part of the evolution legend. Circa 1890. 64" x 47". Courtesy, Dewey Galleries, Ltd.

Large pictorial of a ceremonial woman figure with a mask. Circa 1915. 73" x 50½". Courtesy, Dewey Galleries, Ltd.

Pictorial weaving of a Hopi Kachina mask. 41" x 29". Courtesy, Lynn Trusdell.

Weaving with geometric Klagetoh/ Two Grey Hills style natural and aniline dyed field and pictorial birds with single Yei figure and lightning lines. Circa 1930s. 73″ x 48½″. Courtesy, Lynn Trusdell.

Pictorial weaving of a medicine man figure of natural wool with aniline accents. Circa 1915. 61″ x 35″. Courtesy, Private Collection on permanent loan to Ohio University.

Weaving with two square panels containing a man and a woman in Navajo dress. 1984. 31″ x 18½″. Courtesy Kiva Indian Trading Post.

The heads of a groom (left) and bride (right) flank a standing ceremonial male figure with head-dress and symbolic objects. This is presumably a wedding scene. Woven with natural and aniline dyed homespun wool. Circa 1920-1930. 50″ x 32″. Courtesy, Dewey Galleries, Ltd.

Pictorial weaving with two figures holding ceremonial devices. Circa 1920-30. 53″ x 49″. Courtesy, Dewey Galleries, Ltd.

Pictorial of a standing woman, her sash with loose fringe. Circa 1990. 18½" x 13". Courtesy, Kiva Indian Trading Post.

The tools and figures of a wedding ceremony are depicted in this weaving with the groom (left) and bride (right) shown in head views and a standing female figure. Circa 1915. Woven with natural and aniline dyed wool. 58½" x 40½". Courtesy, Private Collection on permanent loan to Ohio University.

Very unusual pictorial weaving showing the inside of a building during a Navajo wedding ceremony. The bride and groom are depicted with attendants, guest, presents, food, and ceremonial objects. Woven by Shirley John, 1990. 59" x 61". Courtesy, Shiprock Trading Company.

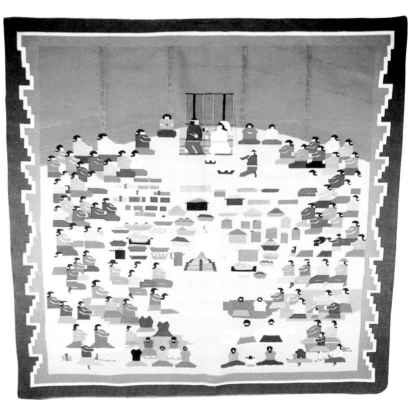

Yei Figures

The Navajo recognize twelve holy persons they call Yei who dance and communicate not with speech but with animal cries.

Very early Yei figures in weaving of simple design with no border. Pre-1920. 16″ x 38″. Courtesy, Crown & Eagle Antiques.

Early Yei figures shown wearing jewelry, no border. Pre-1920. 16″ x 33″. Courtesy, Crown & Eagle Antiques.

Pictorial showing a Plains Indian with headdress. 15″ x 19″. Courtesy, Dewey Galleries, Ltd.

Unusual cross-shaped weaving with male and female dancers, natural and aniline dyed wool. 1920s. 52½" x 44". Courtesy, Dewey Galleries, Ltd.

Pictorial of one male dancer with mask and rattle. Woven by Cynthia George. 16½" x 8½". Courtesy, Shiprock Trading Company.

Pictorial of a lone woman Yei figure. Circa 1945-55. 34" x 51". Courtesy, Dewey Galleries, Ltd.

Pictorial of a large central dancing ceremonial figure with mask and animal tail. Circa 1920-30. 61" x 29". Courtesy, Dewey Galleries, Ltd.

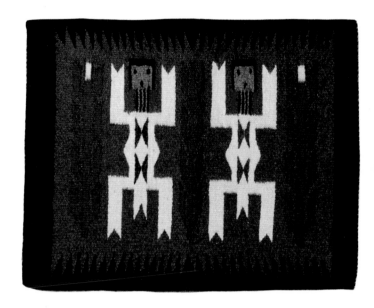

Single Yei figure and corn plants in a borderless design. 33″ x 33″. Courtesy, Dewey Galleries, Ltd.

Pictorial weaving of corn stalks and Yei figures in raised outline technique. Woven by Doris Haskan, 1976. Courtesy, Dennehotso Collection.

Weaving of two Yei figures and three corn plants. Woven by Betty Thompson. 15½″ x 19½″. Courtesy, Foutz Trading Company.

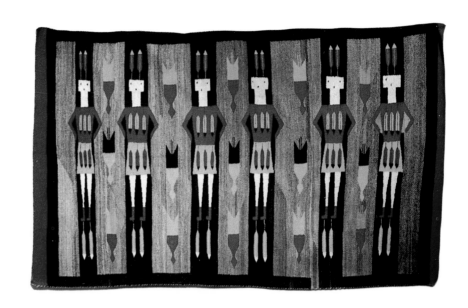

Pictorial Yei design with six figures, natural and aniline dyed wool. 1925. 50" x 83". Courtesy, Dewey Galleries, Ltd.

Pictorial weaving with eight Yei and landscape with rock formations. Woven by Roselyn Begay, 1990. 54½" x 32½". Courtesy, Hogback Trading Post.

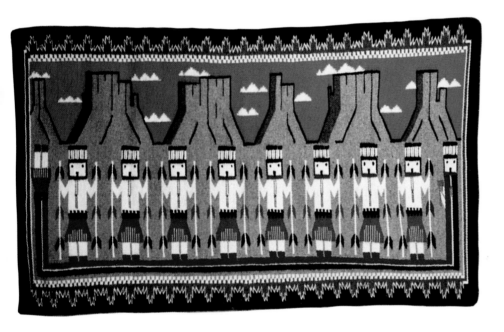

Pictorial Yei design with corn plants and pastel geometric border in Burntwater style with vegetal dyed wool. Woven by Lillian Joe, Shiprock. 35½" x 47". Courtesy, Foutz Trading Company.

Yei dancers designed with great detail, grey background, natural wool. Woven by Ruby White, 1990. 35″ x 47″. Courtesy, Foutz Trading Company.

Two-faced twill weaving with Yei dancing figures and geometric pattern. Woven by Sandra Wilson, Kinlichee, Arizona, 1990. 20″ x 36″. Courtesy, Hubbell Trading Post.

Yei Bi Chei Figures

When the Yei figures (holy persons) dance, only Talking God, or Yei bi chei (maternal grandfather of the Yei), their leader, communicates with human speech. He is shown at the head of the line of dancers in a different dress.

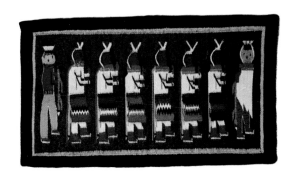

Yei bi chei pictorial. Woven by Ilene Etcitty, 1989. 21" x 37". Courtesy, Foutz Trading Company.

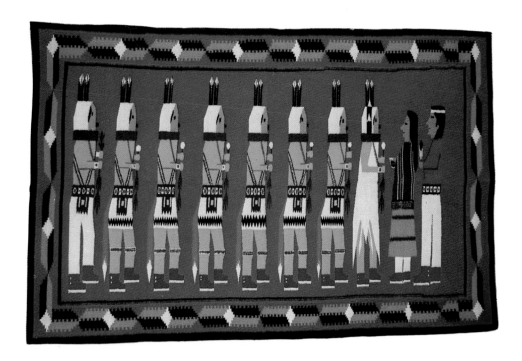

Yei bi chei figures with Navajo couple. Circa 1980. Courtesy, Dennehotso Collection.

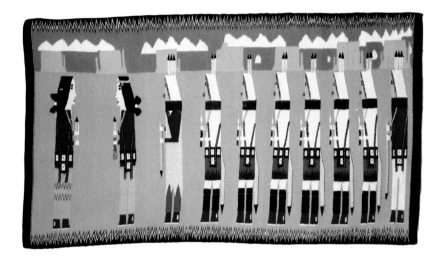

Yei bi chei weaving with landscape background. Woven by Albert Woody, Shiprock, New Mexico. 29" x 50". Courtesy, Hubbell Trading Post.

The Yei dancers are seen performing in this pictorial landscape weaving near the bottom of the design. The detail shown of such a Navajo ceremony is quite remarkable. 49½″ x 38¼″. Courtesy, Private Collection.

Here the Yei bi chei dances at the head of the line in a pictorial landscape of delightful composition. 49″ x 96″. Courtesy, Private Collection.

Trees of Life

Navajo symbols include a medicine basket with corn plant growing from it which conveys the Tree of Life in their religion. Birds often accompany this tree design.

Pictorial Tree of Life with feathers in the borders. Woven by Phyllis Francis, 1976. 55¼" x 39½". Courtesy, Private Collection on permanent loan to Ohio University.

Tree of Life labeled, "Hello". 1990. 15½" x 10". Courtesy, Shiprock Trading Company.

Double Tree of Life and figural pictorial weaving within a bold star design border. Circa 1980. Courtesy, Private Collection.

A Rainbow maiden surrounds a
Tree of Life and landscape design.
Woven by Mary Dick, 1973.
Courtesy, Private Collection.

Two Trees of Life and two additional
baskets with corn and corn meal, of
course the birds are present. Woven
by Lena Cly, Sweetwater, 1973.
Courtesy, Private Collection.

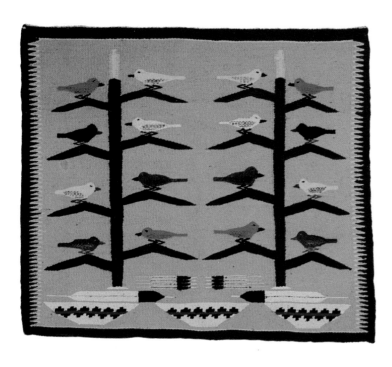

Two Trees of Life with birds and
three baskets. 1984. 28½" x 33".
Courtesy, Private Collection on
permanent loan to Ohio University.

Trees with Birds

Tree with birds pictorial, Germantown wool. Circa 1875-1885. 31" x
22". Courtesy, Dewey Galleries, Ltd.

Pictorial weaving of a corn plant
with birds and two lizards and
unusual arrows in the border. Circa
1910-1920. 72" x 41". Courtesy
Dewey Galleries, Ltd.

Cheerful flowering tree pictorial
weaving of Germantown wool.
Woven about 1911. 23" x 43".
Courtesy Dewey Galleries, Ltd.

Corn plant with birds pictorial weaving within a bold border of feather designs. Circa 1975. Woven by Phyllis Francis. Courtesy, Private Collection.

Corn plant and landscape pictorial weaving. Woven by Virginia Leonard, 1990. 41½" x 22¼". Courtesy, Foutz Trading Company.

Pictorial weaving with three corn plants and birds, a medicine basket on the ground. Woven by Helen Solzar. Circa 1970. Courtesy, Private Collection.

Corn plant pictorial weaving with smaller side plants, birds, and feather design, including natural, vegetal yellow dyed, and aniline dyed wool. Circa 1920-1940. 72" x 48". Courtesy, Private Collection.

Two corn plants/Yei figures with birds, arrows, feathers, and ? caterpillars in a pictorial weaving. Circa 1940. 57" x 42". Courtesy Dewey Galleries, Ltd.

Pictorial weaving with tweed background and corn plant with birds and two rock formations. Woven with commercial yarn and wool warp. Woven by Pauline Nez, Dennehotso, 1974. 20" x 24". Courtesy, Dennehotso Collection.

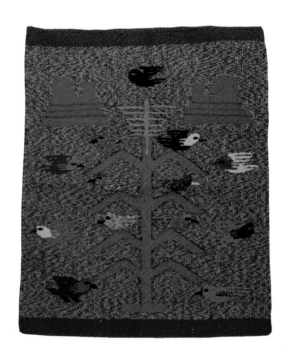

Pine tree with many birds in a pictorial weaving with outlined border. Woven by Rena Mountain, Cedar Ridge, 1990. 48" x 34". Courtesy, Hubbell Trading Post.

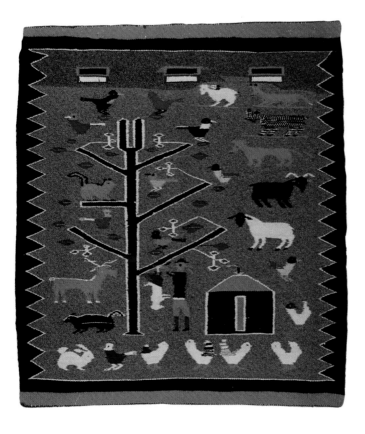

Pictorial landscape with tree supporting birds, a squirrel, and hanging carcas within a farm yard. Woven by Ann Tsosie, Teec Nos Pos, 1976. 33" x 29". Courtesy, Private Collection.

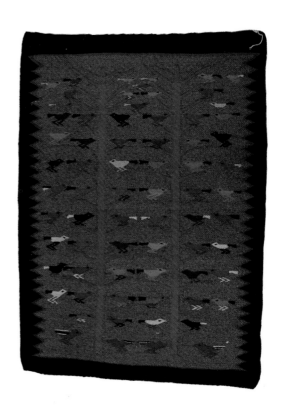

Pictorial weaving of multi-colored birds on two corn stalks within an outlined border. Woven by Stella Begay. Courtesy, Private Collection.

Sandpaintings

Navajo religious healing ceremonies often include sacred designs executed in colored sand on the earth floor of a Navajo home. These designs symbolize different aspects of the gods, and are known as Sandpaintings. Many still consider it tabu to represent the Sandpaintings in any permanent form, such as weavings.

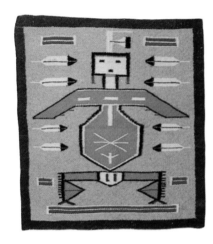

Single sandpainting style Yei figure with feathers. 25¼" x 22¾". Courtesy, Private Collection.

Single sandpainting style Yei figure. Circa 1920s. 61" x 43". Courtesy, Dewey Galleries, Ltd.

Pictorial weaving depicting a healing ceremony inside a Navajo home. Here the colored sands and tools to make a sandpainting are shown. Woven by Valencia Nez. 37" x 49½". Courtesy, Shiprock Trading Company.

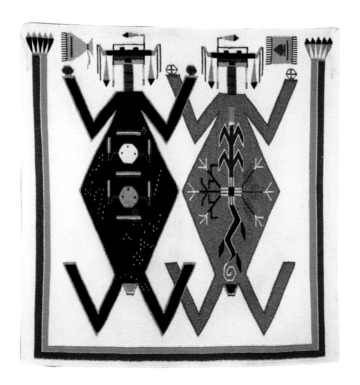

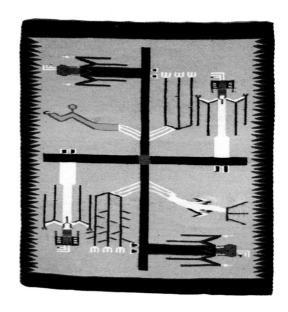

Weaving with a sandpainting design in four squares including a whirling logo cross motif. Woven by Reba Gilmore, Chinle. 39" x 39½". Courtesy, Hubbell Trading Post.

Pictorial weaving of the sandpainting representations of Mother Earth (right) and Father Sky (left). Woven by Brenda Crosby, 1990. 36" x 35". Courtesy, Hogback Trading Post.

Weaving showing a sandpainting design with four frogs from the Beautyway chant and pictorial birds and butterflies. Courtesy, Foutz Trading Company.

Sandpainting design with four snakes and three Yei figures within a Rainbow Yei border. Woven by Sadie Ross, Red Rock, New Mexico. 42″ x 53″. Courtesy, Hubbell Trading Post.

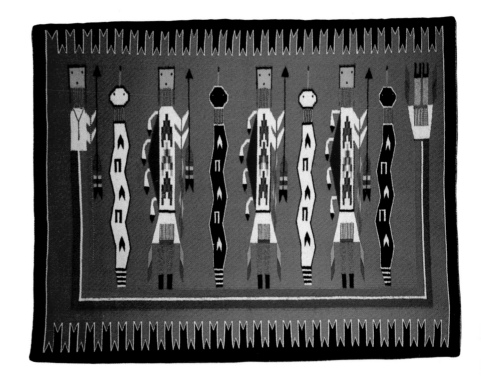

Sandpainting design of a Rainbow Yei, four corn maidens (blue), and the four plants sacred to the Navajo: corn, beans, squash, and tobacco. Woven by Rita Gilmore, Chinle/ Cedar Ridge. 35″ x 49″. Courtesy, Hubbell Trading Post.

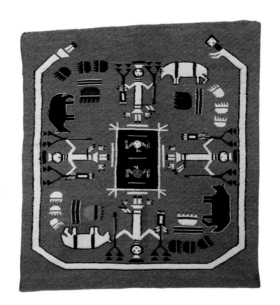

Sandpainting design of bear tracks and the four seasons in a pictorial. Woven by Sadie Ross, Red Rock, New Mexico, 1990. 37″ x 36″. Courtesy, Foutz Trading Company.

MULTIPLE DESIGNS

Ambitious weavers capable of designing more than one regional design once in a while make a multiple patterned weaving to demonstrate their skill. Most of these are Four-In-One designs, but occasionally these are Five-, Six-, Eight-, Nine-In-One and more. These are among the rarest Navajo weavings of the contemporary types.

Four-In-One pictorial weaving including Reservation Roads, medicine baskets, Tree of Life, and landscape designs, fine weaving. 17½" x 19½". Courtesy, Private Collection.

Multiple weaving in a Storm Pattern with the "four corners" states, Utah, Colorado, Arizona and New Mexico depicted, and four animals in the corners. Woven by Nellie N. Lee, 1973. Courtesy, Dennehotso Collection.

Two-In-One multiple weaving of commercial yarn showing two landscape designs. Woven by Joanna Goat, 1973. 26" x 31". Courtesy, Dennehotso Collection.

Storm Pattern and Five-In-One multiple weaving of animals and landscape designs. Woven by Gladys Richards. Courtesy, Private Collection.

Multiple pictorial weaving with "four corners" blocks and four animals with many pictorial images. Woven by Susie Yazzie Whitesheep. Courtesy, Dennehotso Collection.

Unusual multiple weaving within a Rainbow Yei design, central "Fire Dancers" and four landscape designs. Woven by Gladys Richards. Courtesy, Private Collection.

Two-faced

Intricately constructed weavings with entirely different designs on the front and back sides are known as Two-Faced weavings. Because of the extra wool carried to make each design, these are quite heavy. Few weavers attempt two-faced projects, so very few are ever available.

Two-faced weaving. Side one: Tree of Life. Side two: Storm Pattern geometric. Circa 1975. Woven by Edna(?). Courtesy, Private Collection.

Two-faced weaving. Side one: horizontal bands. Side two: landscape pictorial. Circa 1975. Woven by Jean Ann Goat. Courtesy, Private Collection.